Perfect Phrases in
American Sign
Language for **Beginners**

Perfect Phrases in **American Sign Language** for **Beginners**

150 ESSENTIAL PHRASES
FOR COMMUNICATING WITH USERS OF ASL

•

Lou Fant
and
Barbara Bernstein Fant

•

Illustrations by Betty G. Miller

McGraw Hill

New York Chicago San Francisco Lisbon London Madrid Mexico City
Milan New Delhi San Juan Seoul Singapore Sydney Toronto

Library of Congress Cataloging-in-Publication Data

Fant, Louie J.
   Perfect phrases in American Sign Language for beginners / Lou Fant and
Barbara Bernstein Fant ; illustrations by Betty G. Miller.
      p.   cm.
   Includes index.
   0-07-159877-4 (alk. paper)
   1. American Sign Language.

HV2475 .F37   2008
419'.7—dc22   2008012718

3 4 5 6 7 8 9 10 11 12 13 14 15 16 17 18 19 20 21 22   QFR/QFR   1 5 4 3 2

ISBN   978-0-07-159877-4
MHID   0-07-159877-4

The publisher would like to thank Darren Fudenske and Melanie Schneider for their help.

McGraw-Hill books are available at special quantity discounts to use as premiums and
sales promotions or for use in corporate training programs. To contact a representative,
please visit the Contact Us pages at www.mhprofessional.com.

This book is printed on acid-free paper.

Contents

Preface

This book is designed to provide various phrases for beginning learners of American Sign Language or those who wish to communicate with the Deaf. American Sign Language is the dominant sign language of the Deaf community in the United States and English-speaking parts of Canada. Here are some key phrases for everyday communication concerning greetings, introductions, signing and deafness, health, numbers, time, money, and more—in short, basic survival phrases in American Sign Language.

This book is not meant to teach the fundamentals of ASL grammar or offer a comprehensive array of phrases (longer discussions of ASL grammar and basics can be found elsewhere, and almost 500 phrases can be found in *The American Sign Language Phrase Book, Third Edition*). Even so, those who consistently use these basic phrases may discover that they begin to understand some sign concepts and can build upon this foundation to continue learning American Sign Language.

It is important to be aware that American Sign is a visual-spatial language distinct from spoken English. It has its own grammar, and the order in which signs are put together is different from English. ASL grammar incorporates not only the use of facial expressions but head and body movements and the efficient use of space around the signer as well.

Acknowledgments

I wish to convey my heartfelt appreciation to Dave A. Morrison, my dear friend and colleague at Seattle Central Community College, for his spirited perusal of this book and suggested changes

I extend my gratitude once more to Holly McGuire at McGraw-Hill for her guidance and assistance on this project.

And to my mother, Rita Bernstein, thank you for the life lessons you have taught me. All my love to you.

Perfect Phrases in **American Sign Language** for **Beginners**

Chapter 1

Basic Sentence Types

As I mentioned earlier in the Introduction chapter, facial expressions play a very significant role in ASL. In a spoken language, the rise and fall of the voice adds meaning to the words spoken. Imagine the various ways one can say "I love you." The characteristic rising of the voice toward the end of a question is another example. Facial expressions are to ASL as vocal inflection is to spoken English.

Throughout this book, you will note that the phrases are delineated as statements or questions. The face has these duties and supplies additional subtleties and nuances of meaning. Signs have meanings in and of themselves just as words do, but these meanings are altered, shaped, enriched, and amplified by facial expressions. This is true especially when one asks questions in ASL. In general, when one asks a *wh-* sign (who, what, why, where, when, which, how, and how many or how much—see Chapter 2), the eyebrows are downward. All other questions usually cause the eyebrows to move upward—for example, questions that require an affirmative or negative response. To support an affirmative response, nodding of the head would occur, e.g., "Yes, I'm married," or a shaking of the head with the "I'm not married" response.

For a *wh-* sign question, the eyebrows usually go downward. The *wh-* sign question is also accompanied by a head tilt.

Eyebrows move upward for other questions and are usually accompanied by a head tilt.

Chapter 2

Question Signs

The *wh-* sign may come at the beginning or at the end of a question, or it may appear in both places. If you wish to emphasize a question, place it at the end.

WHO

WHAT SHRUG

WHAT

WHY

WHERE

WHEN

WHICH

HOW

HOW MANY/HOW MUCH

Chapter 3

Greetings, Introductions, and Common Expressions

Hello.

HELLO

Good morning.

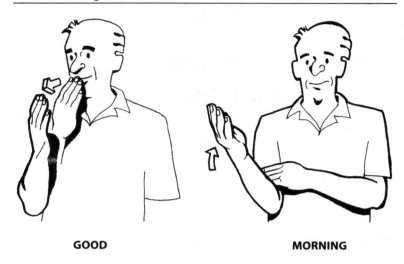

GOOD MORNING

Good afternoon.

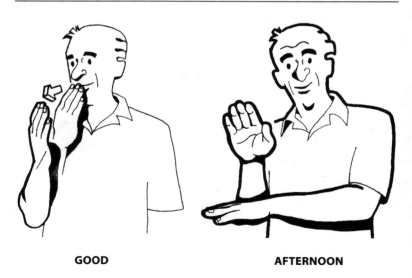

GOOD AFTERNOON

Good night.

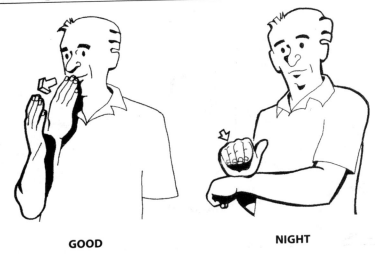

GOOD   **NIGHT**

I'm glad to see you.

HAPPY   **SEE**

Good-bye.

GOOD-BYE

Please.

PLEASE

Yes.

YES

No.

NO

Thank you.

GOOD

Excuse me.

EXCUSE

It's all right. It's okay.

ALL RIGHT

I'm sorry.

SORRY

What is your name?

NAME   WHAT SHRUG

My name is _____.

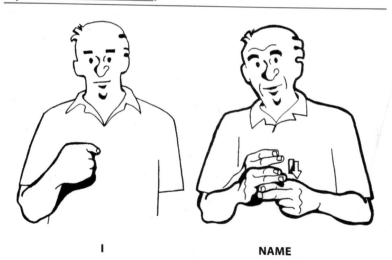

I   NAME

Fingerspell your name.

It's nice to meet you.

NICE

MEET

Where do you live?

LIVE

WHERE

Where are you from?

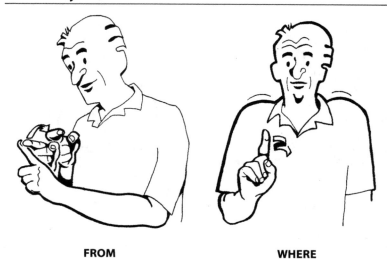

FROM   **WHERE**

Are you in school?

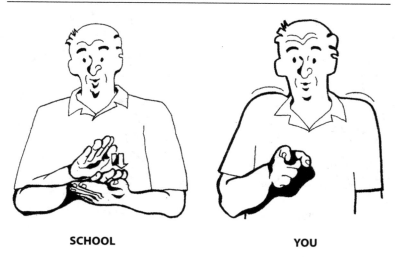

SCHOOL   **YOU**

I'm a student.

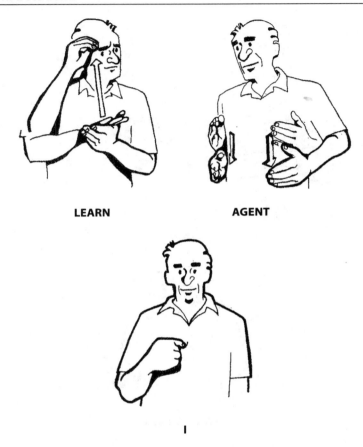

LEARN   AGENT

I

AGENT is a sign used in conjunction with another sign in order to designate a person who does a particular thing. The AGENT sign can be used with most but not all occupations

What kind of work do you do?

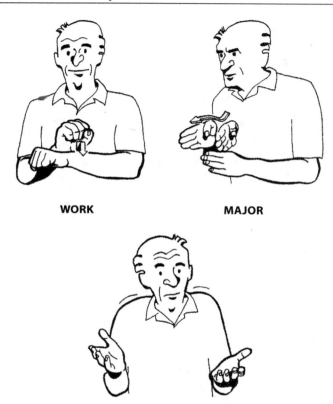

WORK

MAJOR

WHAT SHRUG

I'm a doctor.

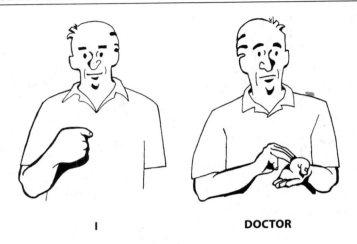

I   DOCTOR

I'm a lawyer/teacher.

LAW   TEACH

He knows me.

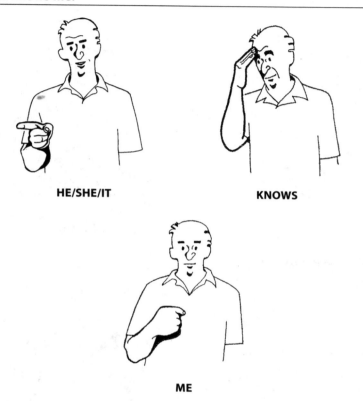

HE/SHE/IT   **KNOWS**

ME

Verbs in ASL fall into three categories: nondirectional verbs, one-directional verbs, and multidirectional verbs. Movement in verb signs may express who is performing an action (the subject) and to whom the action is directed (the direct object). This quality of movement is called verb directionality

The nondirectional verbs (like the one above) do not express either subject or direct object; therefore, these two things (subject and direct object nouns and pronouns) must be supplied.

I love you.

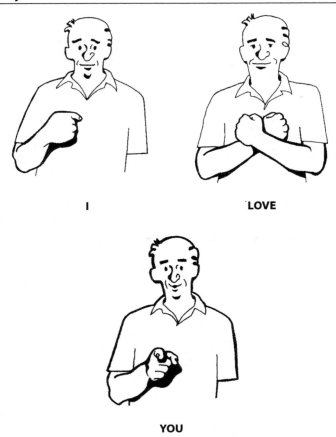

I   LOVE

YOU

This is also a nondirectional verb.

I see him/her/it.

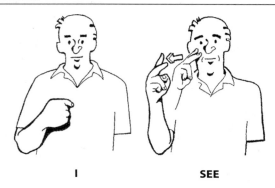

I   SEE

In regard to verb directionality, as seen in this example one-directional verb signs express direct object but not subject; that is, one-directional verbs move toward the direct object; thus, a noun or pronoun is not required.

I help you.

HELP

Here we see an example of a multidirectional verb sign in which the movement goes from the subject toward the direct object; thus, neither subject nor direct object is signed.

You tell me.

YOU

TELL ME

This is another one-directional verb sign.

Can you give me the time?

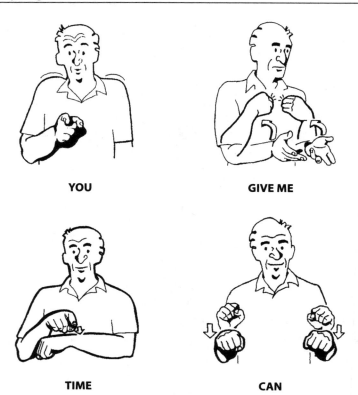

YOU

GIVE ME

TIME

CAN

Chapter 4

Getting Better Acquainted

How are you?

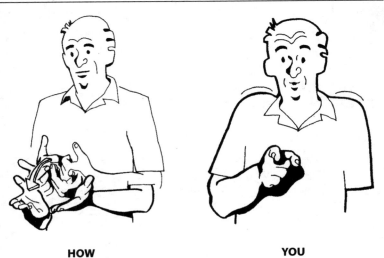

HOW   YOU

Fine.

FINE

Additional vocabulary:

I am sick/tired/wonderful.

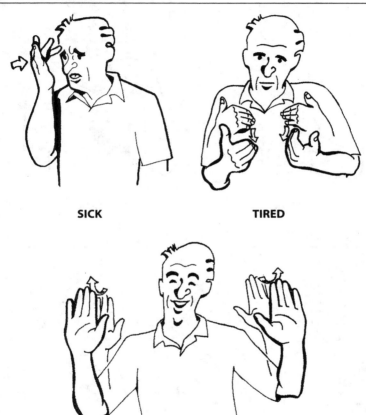

SICK   **TIRED**

WONDERFUL

Are you married?

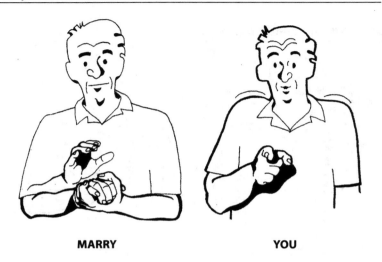

MARRY   YOU

Yes, I'm married.

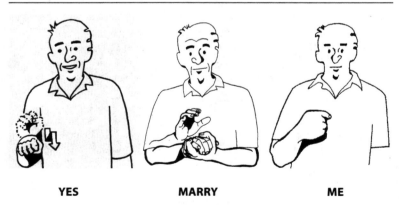

YES   MARRY   ME

May I introduce my wife?

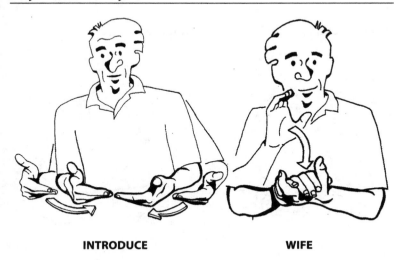

INTRODUCE   WIFE

Additional vocabulary:

May I introduce my husband/son/daughter/friend?

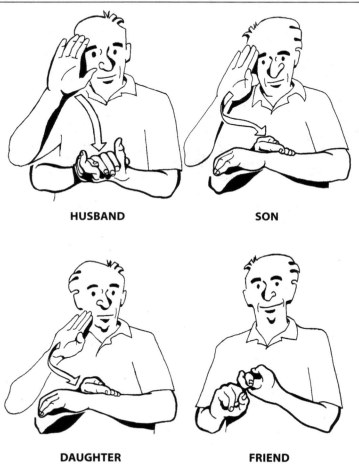

HUSBAND	**SON**
DAUGHTER	**FRIEND**

After making the sign for the person you are introducing, you then fingerspell that person's name.

I'm single.

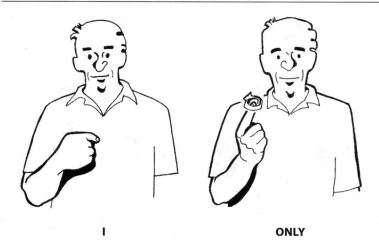

I   ONLY

I'm divorced.

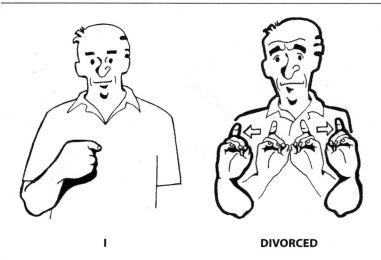

I   DIVORCED

Do you have any children?

CHILDREN   HAVE

YOU

Have you eaten? Did you eat? Are you finished eating?

EAT   **FINISH**

35

I haven't eaten yet.

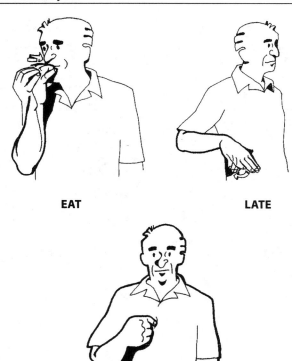

EAT   LATE

I

Are you hungry?

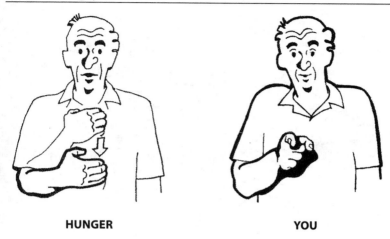

HUNGER   YOU

Let's you and I go to a restaurant.

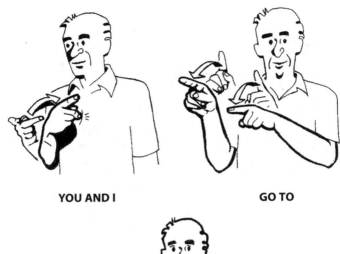

YOU AND I   GO TO

RESTAURANT

What are you going to order?

ORDER   WHAT SHRUG

I will order breakfast.

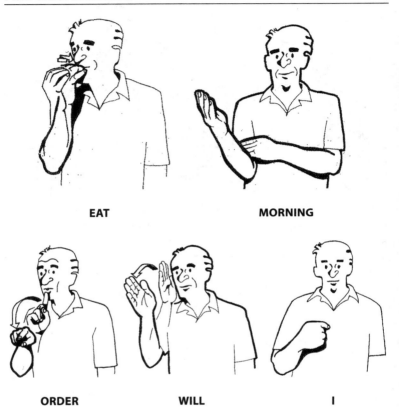

EAT   MORNING

ORDER   WILL   I

Lunch/dinner

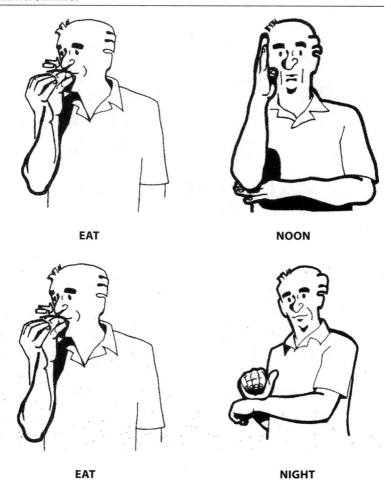

EAT

NOON

EAT

NIGHT

She can't go.

WOMAN   GO TO

CAN'T   HE/SHE/IT

Do you have a car?

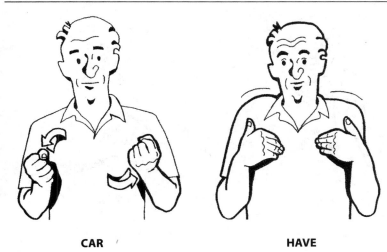

CAR

HAVE

May I go with you?

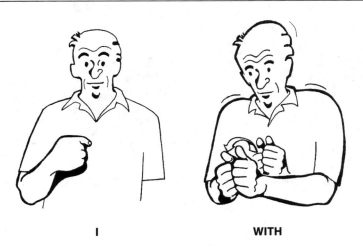

I

WITH

Come visit me sometime.

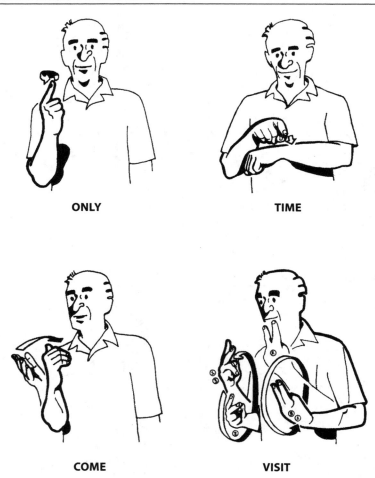

ONLY

TIME

COME

VISIT

Chapter 5

Signing and Deafness

I'm learning sign language.

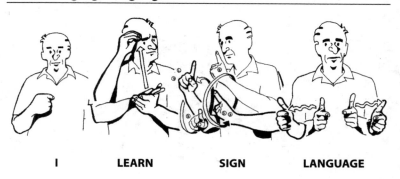

| I | LEARN | SIGN | LANGUAGE |

Sign slowly, please.

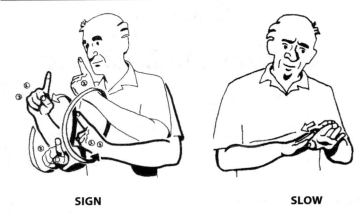

SIGN   SLOW

PLEASE

Please repeat.

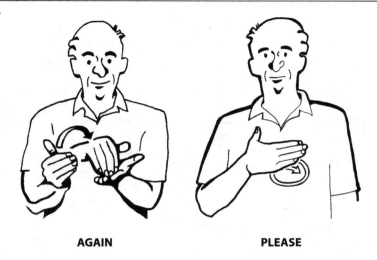

AGAIN   PLEASE

I can fingerspell, but I can't read it well.

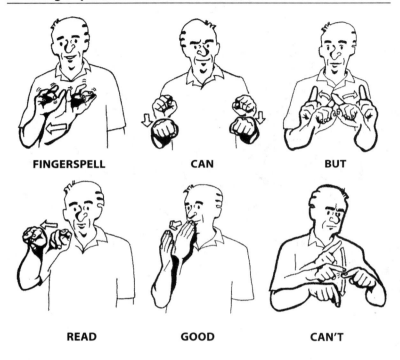

FINGERSPELL	CAN	BUT

READ	GOOD	CAN'T

You sign fast.

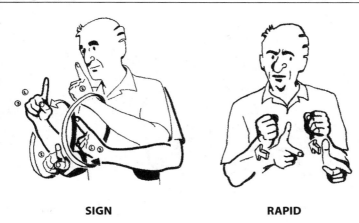

SIGN   **RAPID**

YOU

I understand.

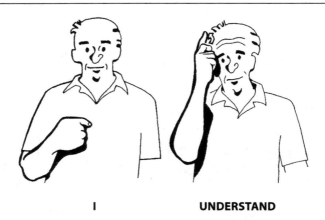

I   UNDERSTAND

I don't understand.

UNDERSTAND

Would you write it, please?

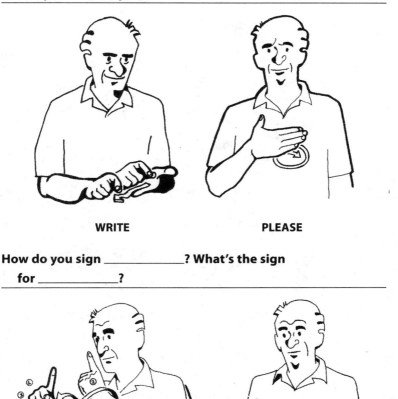

WRITE

PLEASE

How do you sign _____? What's the sign
for _____?

SIGN

HOW

Ask these questions by pointing to whatever it is you want to know the sign for or by fingerspelling the word.

There's no sign for that; you have to fingerspell it.

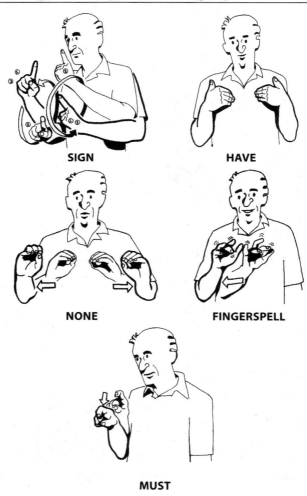

SIGN

HAVE

NONE

FINGERSPELL

MUST

What does _____ mean?

MEAN

WHAT SHRUG

To ask this question, first make the sign of whatever it is that you want to know the meaning of, then sign MEAN WHAT SHRUG.

Are you deaf?

DEAF (A)   DEAF (B)

YOU

Either way of signing "deaf" is acceptable.

I'm not deaf; I'm hearing.

DEAF   NOT

SPEAK   I

I'm hard of hearing.

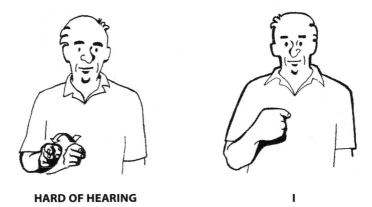

HARD OF HEARING   I

Do you use a hearing aid?

HEARING AID   **USE**

YOU

Can you read lips?

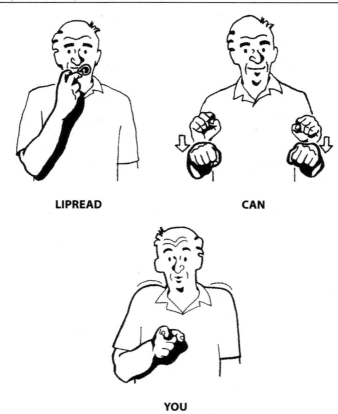

LIPREAD   **CAN**

YOU

I speak a little.

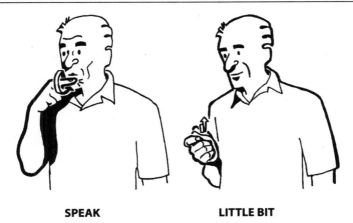

SPEAK   LITTLE BIT

I was born deaf.

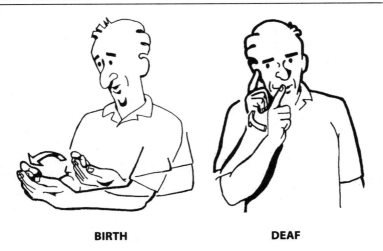

BIRTH   DEAF

Chapter 6

Health

How do you feel?

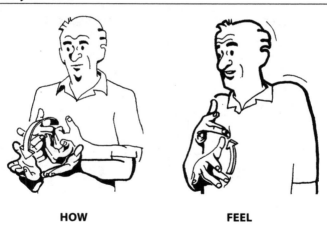

HOW   FEEL

Do you feel all right?

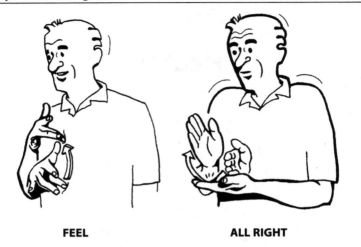

FEEL   **ALL RIGHT**

I don't feel well.

FEEL   **GOOD**

NOT

I am sick.

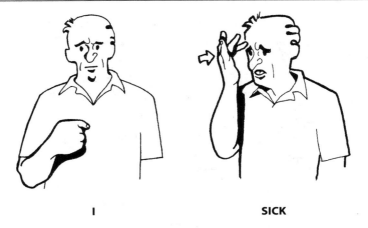

I   SICK

I am really sick.

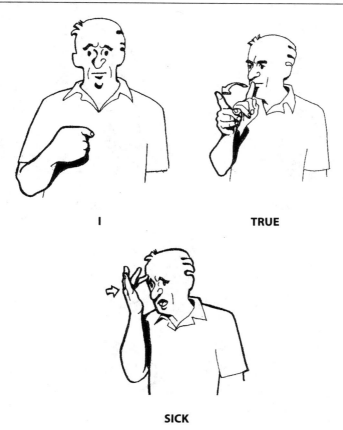

I   TRUE

SICK

When the signer wishes to stress or emphasize statements, then the TRUE sign is used.

I feel better now.

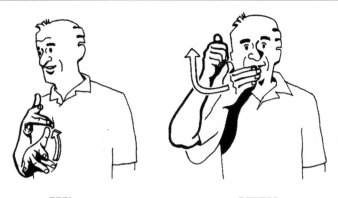

FEEL   BETTER

NOW

Where is the rest room?

TOILET

WHERE

Wash your hands.

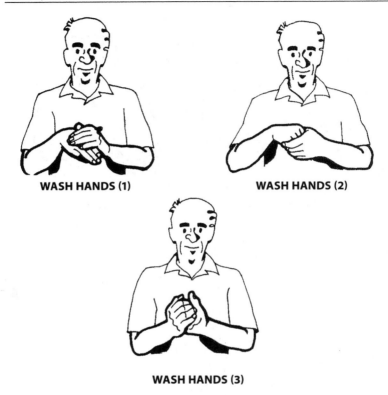

WASH HANDS (1)   **WASH HANDS (2)**

WASH HANDS (3)

This sign, shown in three steps, is a mime of actually washing the hands.

Wash your face.

WASH FACE

Similarly, this sign is a mime of actually washing the face.

Where does it hurt?

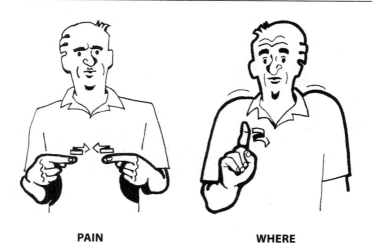

PAIN   WHERE

My head aches.

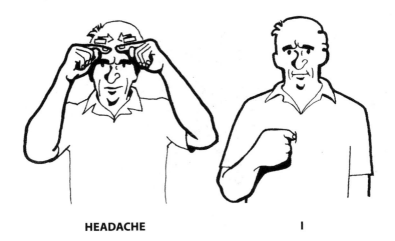

HEADACHE   **I**

I have a toothache.

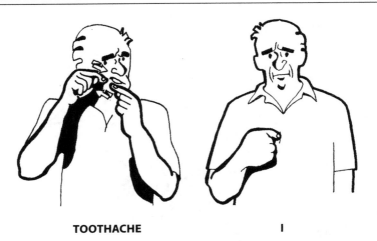

TOOTHACHE   **I**

I have a stomachache.

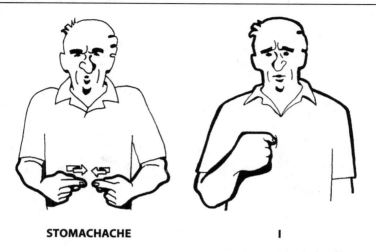

STOMACHACHE   **I**

The sign PAIN may be placed anywhere on the body to denote that you are hurt or have a pain in that part of your body.

I have a cold.

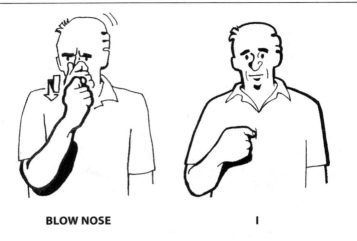

BLOW NOSE   **I**

Do you have any aspirin?

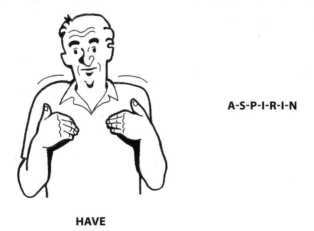

A-S-P-I-R-I-N

HAVE

Fingerspell ASPIRIN.

I need a dentist/doctor.

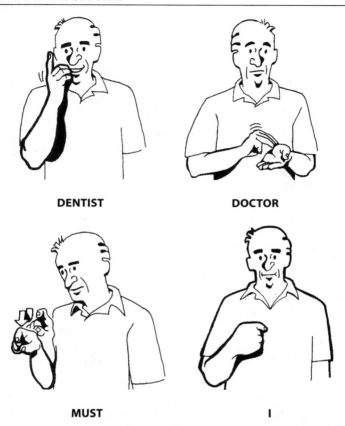

DENTIST **DOCTOR**

MUST **I**

I have to take pills.

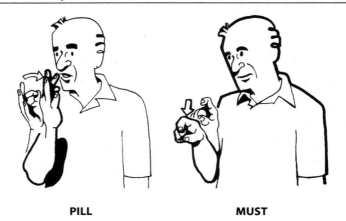

PILL   MUST

I've run out of medicine.

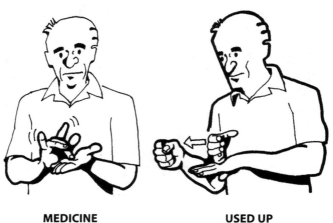

MEDICINE   USED UP

It's time to take your temperature.

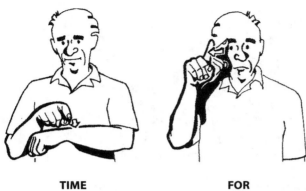

TIME   FOR

ORAL THERMOMETER

You have to have a shot.

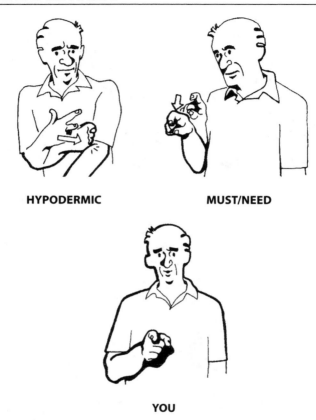

HYPODERMIC   MUST/NEED

YOU

The MUST sign may mean "need" or "should" and is done differently depending on the meaning desired. If something is mandatory, then make one movement down. If something is optional but desirable, then make two gentle downward movements.

You need to have an X-ray.

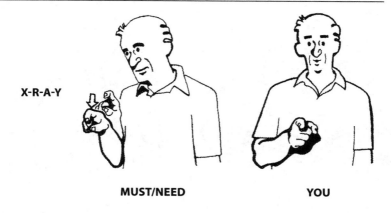

X-R-A-Y

MUST/NEED

YOU

Fingerspell X-RAY.

Were any bones broken?

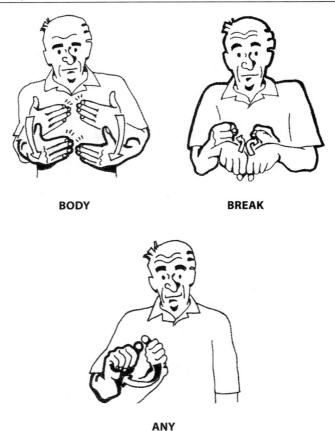

BODY   BREAK

ANY

There is no standard sign for "bone," so the statement here is more generally read as, "Is anything in your body broken?" If you wish to sign "bone" specifically, you must fingerspell it or find out what the local sign for it is.

Call the ambulance.

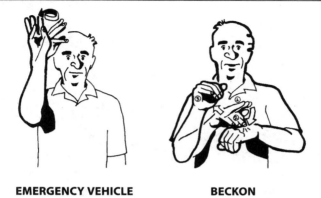

EMERGENCY VEHICLE   **BECKON**

The sign for "ambulance" indicates the spinning red light on top of the vehicle and may refer to any emergency vehicle or just the flashing red light itself.

My wife is in the hospital.

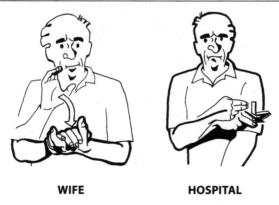

WIFE   **HOSPITAL**

Any family member or friends sign can be substituted in lieu of WIFE to create new phrases. The HOSPITAL sign is made by drawing a cross on the sleeve.

Do you have hospitalization insurance?

HOSPITAL   INSURANCE

HAVE

Chapter 7

Numbers, Time, Dates, and Money

See Chapter 10 for additional vocabulary in numbers, time, and money.

What's your phone number?

PHONE   **NUMBER**   **WHAT SHRUG**

My phone number is _____.

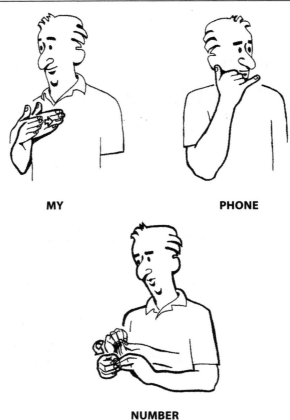

MY   PHONE

NUMBER

Fingerspell your phone number after the sign NUMBER. (See Chapter 10 for number signs.)

What time is it?

TIME

It is 4:45.

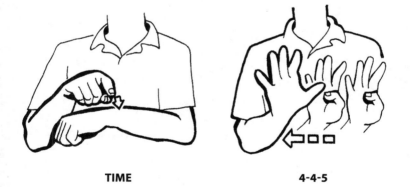

TIME   **4-4-5**

It is 6:15.

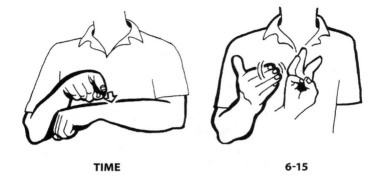

TIME   6-15

I have an appointment at 2:30.

APPOINTMENT   TIME

2-30

How old are you?

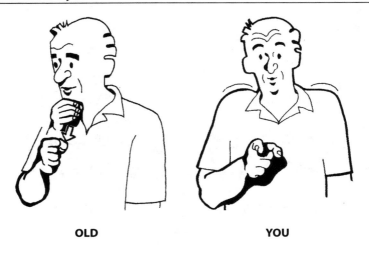

OLD   YOU

He is 87 years old.

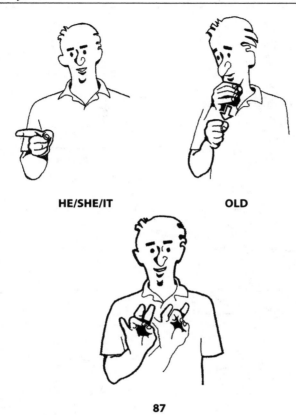

HE/SHE/IT   **OLD**

87

My birthday is April 3, 1948.

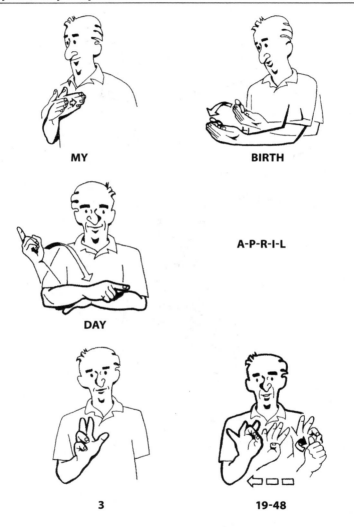

MY

BIRTH

A-P-R-I-L

DAY

3

19-48

The months of March, April, May, June, and July are spelled out. Months with more letters are abbreviated in fingerspelling.

I'll see you next Monday.

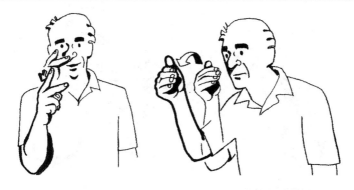

SEE   NEAR FUTURE

MONDAY

He goes to the movies every Tuesday.

EVERY TUESDAY

GO TO

MOVIE

HE/SHE/IT

By moving the sign for a day of the week downward, as done with TUESDAY here, you convey the idea of every week on that day.

I see her every Saturday.

EVERY SATURDAY   **SEE**

I visited my aunt two months ago.

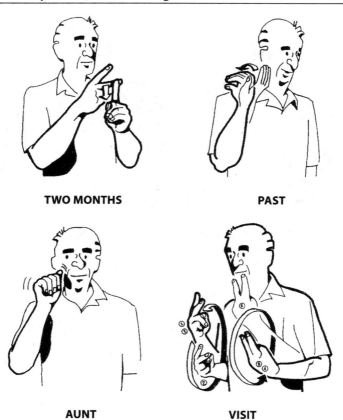

TWO MONTHS

PAST

AUNT

VISIT

I bought a new house two years ago.

TWO YEARS AGO

BUY

NEW

HOUSE

I graduate in two years.

TWO YEARS FROM NOW   **GRADUATE**

I

I pay every three months.

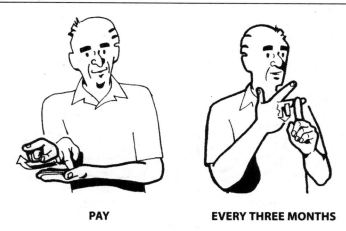

PAY　　　　　　　　**EVERY THREE MONTHS**

How much does the book cost?

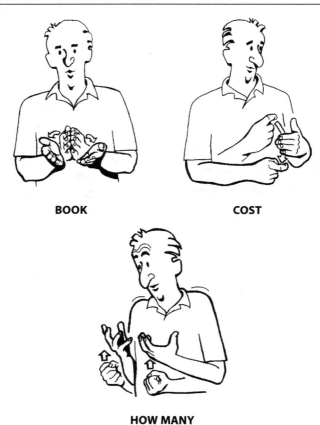

BOOK

COST

HOW MANY

How much did you pay?

PAY　　　　　　　　HOW MANY

Have you a nickel/dime/quarter?

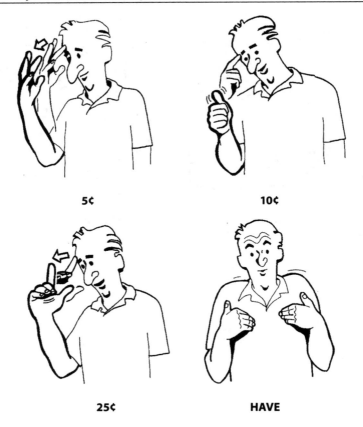

5¢

10¢

25¢

HAVE

I have no money.

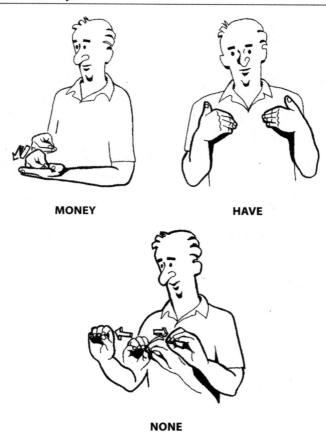

MONEY

HAVE

NONE

I'm broke.

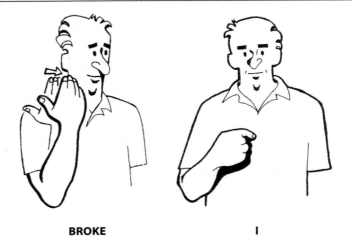

BROKE   I

How much does she owe?

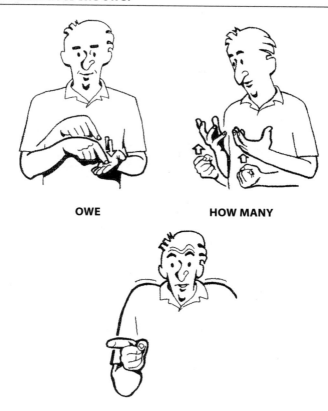

OWE

HOW MANY

HE/SHE/IT

Chapter 8

Technology

Would you mind giving me your e-mail address?

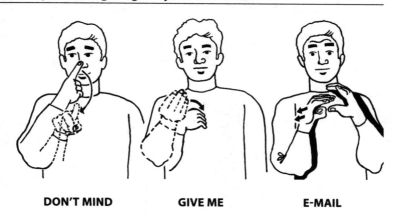

DON'T MIND GIVE ME E-MAIL

I need to recharge my mobile phone.

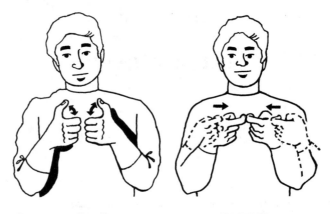

MOBILE PHONE   **PLUG IN**

MUST/NEED

Mine's a BlackBerry/phone.

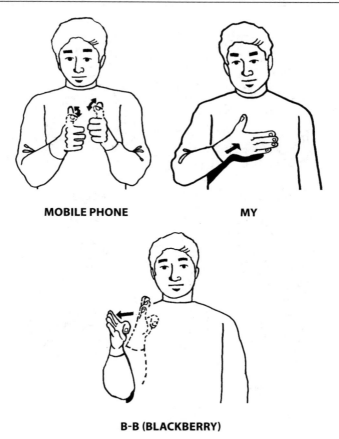

MOBILE PHONE **MY**

B-B (BLACKBERRY)

Fingerspell "B-B."

Deaf people text message their hearing friends.

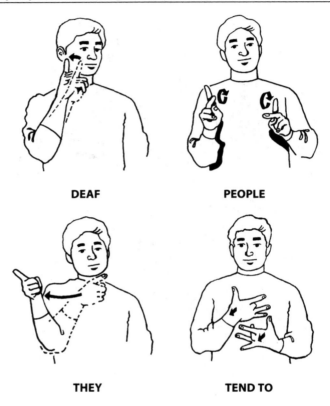

DEAF

PEOPLE

THEY

TEND TO

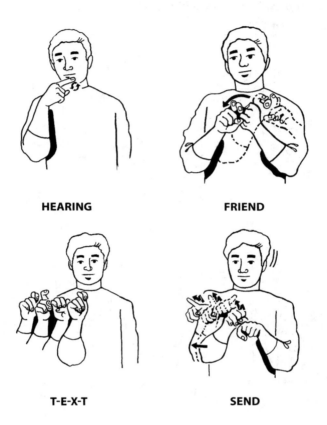

HEARING

FRIEND

T-E-X-T

SEND

Fingerspell "TEXT."

Most deaf people are using video relay services rather than TTYs.

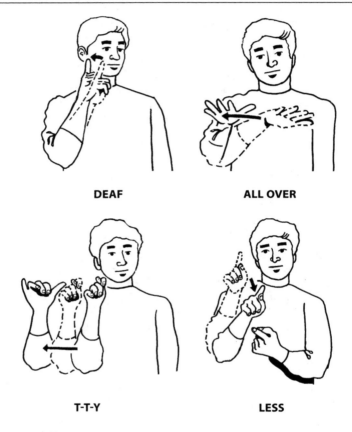

DEAF   ALL OVER

T-T-Y   LESS

Fingerspell "T-T-Y."

NOW   **VIDEO RELAY**

When you get home, check your video relay mail.

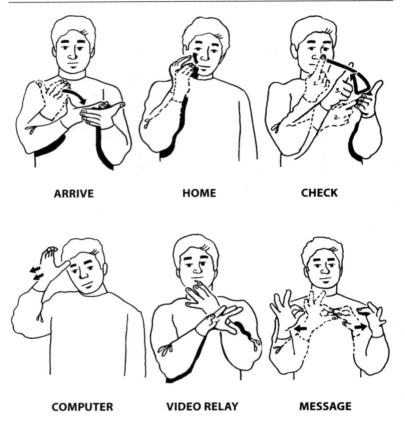

ARRIVE   HOME   CHECK

COMPUTER   VIDEO RELAY   MESSAGE

There are many different signs for computer (see also page 114).

My TV has closed captioning.

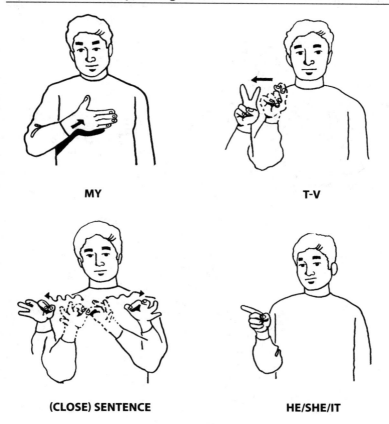

MY

T-V

(CLOSE) SENTENCE

HE/SHE/IT

Fingerspell "T-V."

He/she has a high-definition TV.

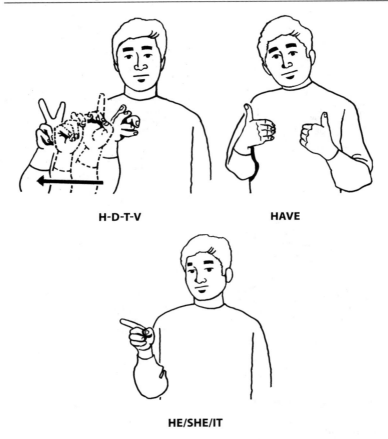

H-D-T-V

HAVE

HE/SHE/IT

Fingerspell "H-D-T-V."

Where's the remote?

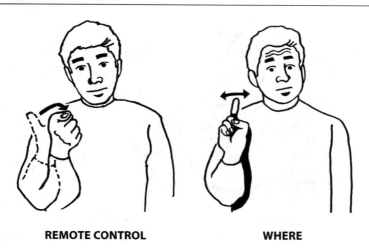

REMOTE CONTROL   **WHERE**

What make is your computer?

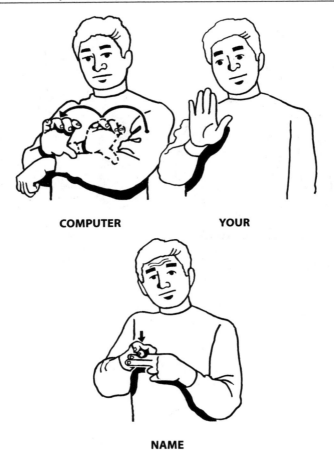

COMPUTER

YOUR

NAME

Note this sign for computer.

Download this program.

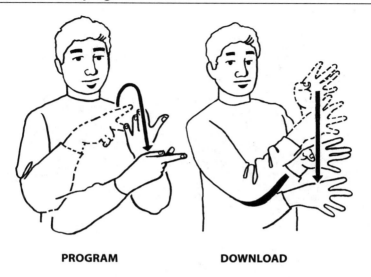

PROGRAM   DOWNLOAD

Please save your file.

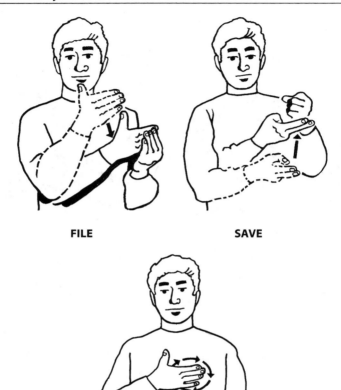

FILE   SAVE

PLEASE

Chapter 9

Holidays and Occasions

Happy birthday.

| HAPPY | BIRTH | DAY |

Have a nice Thanksgiving.

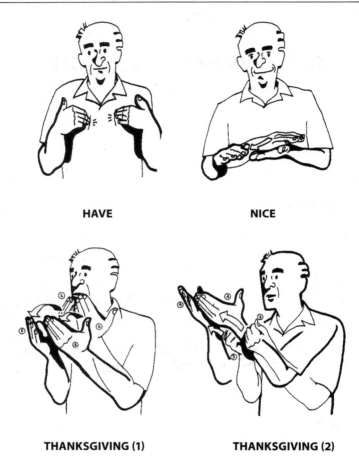

HAVE

NICE

THANKSGIVING (1)

THANKSGIVING (2)

Merry Christmas.

HAPPY   CHRISTMAS

Note: for Christmas Eve, the word *Eve* is fingerspelled.

Happy New Year.

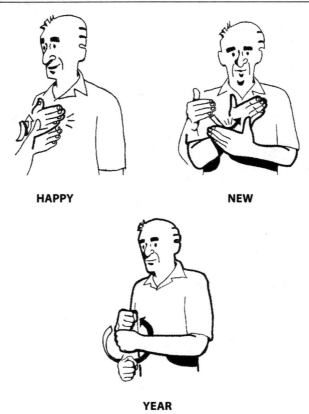

HAPPY

NEW

YEAR

Note: For New Year's Eve, the word *Eve* is fingerspelled.

Happy Passover.

HAPPY   **CRACKER (PASSOVER)**

Happy Hanukkah.

HAPPY   **HANNUKAH**

Happy Fourth of July.

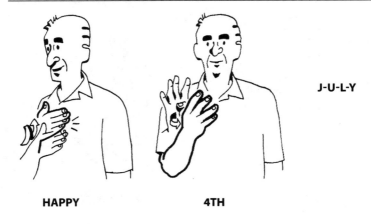

J-U-L-Y

HAPPY   **4TH**

Fingerspell JULY.

Chapter 10
Additional Vocabulary

Miscellaneous Key Vocabulary

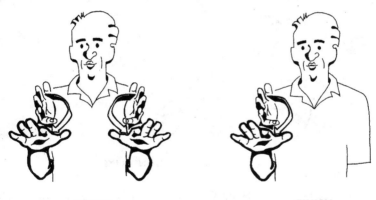

FINISH   FINISH

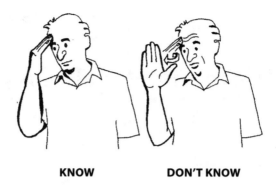

KNOW   **DON'T KNOW**

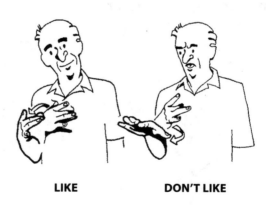

LIKE   **DON'T LIKE**

These three verb signs (KNOW, LIKE, and WANT) have negation built into them. The signer should always shake the head while simultaneously making the negative form of the sign.

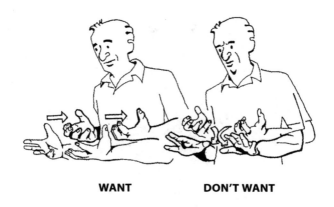

WANT   DON'T WANT

Pronouns

I/ME

YOU

HE/SHE/IT

THEY

MY

HIS/HER/ITS

YOUR

OUR

THEIR

Family Signs

Our family is large/small.

OUR   FAMILY

LARGE   SMALL

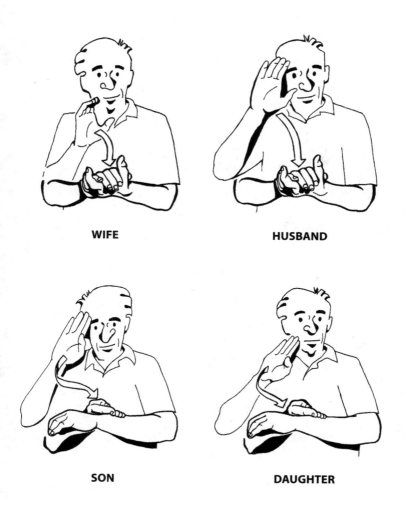

WIFE

HUSBAND

SON

DAUGHTER

FRIEND

FATHER

MOTHER

BROTHER

SISTER

MAN

WOMAN

GIRL

BOY

AUNT

UNCLE

Numbers

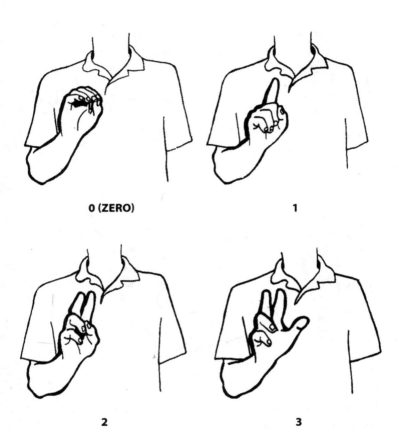

0 (ZERO)

1

2

3

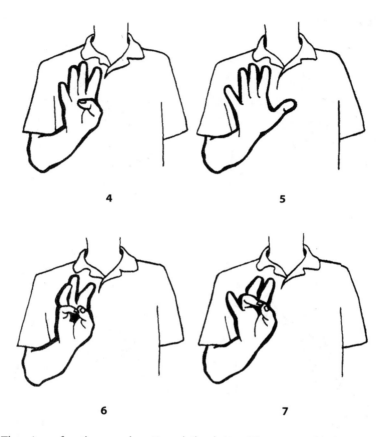

The signs for the number 6 and the letter *W* are exactly the same. Context tells you whether the number or the letter is intended.

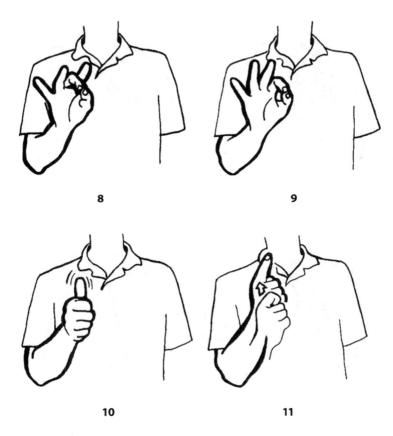

8   9

10   11

The sign for the number 9 is the same as that for the letter *F*.

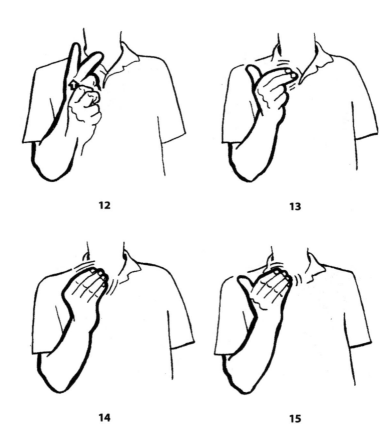

12

13

14

15

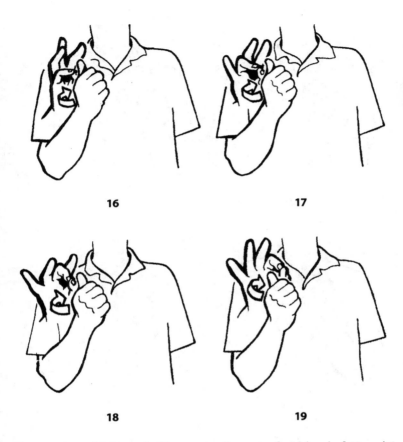

The numbers 16 through 19 are actually a very fast blend of 10 and 6, 10 and 7, 10 and 8, and 10 and 9.

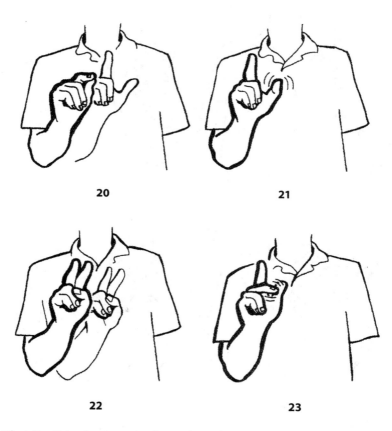

20

21

22

23

That the 2 in the twenties is made with the thumb and index finger rather than the index and middle finger—as it appears in the number 22—is probably due to the fact that ASL has its roots in the old French sign language. In Europe, even hearing people count *one* with the thumb and *two* with the thumb and index finger.

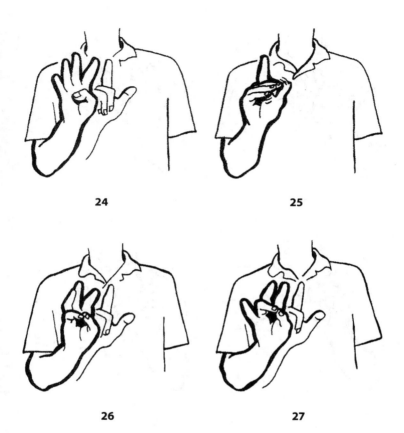

24   25

26   27

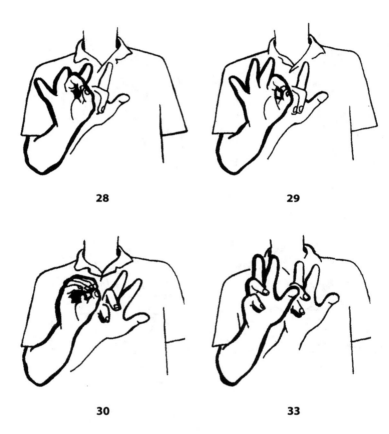

28

29

30

33

The numbers from 30 through 99 are done with the numbers 0 through 9.

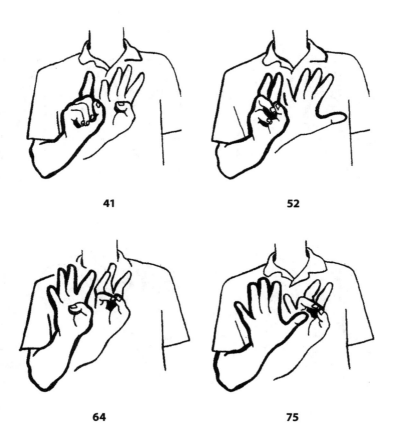

41   52

64   75

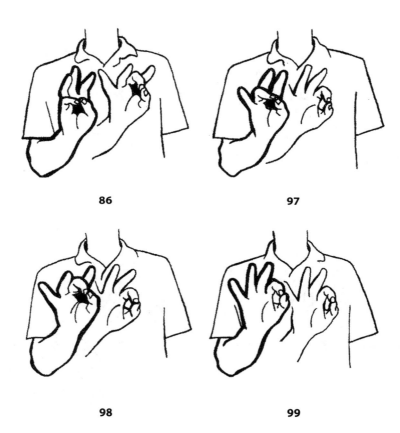

86

97

98

99

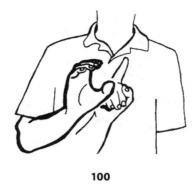

100

The number 100 is made by signing the number 1 and the letter C.

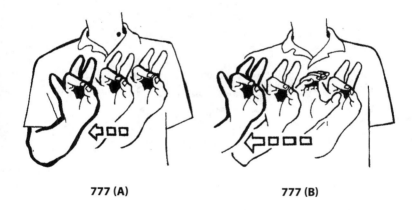

777 (A)   **777 (B)**

The numbers between 100 and 999 are made in one of two ways. One may make the number "7-7-7" or one may sign "7-C-7-7":

1,000

1,000,000

Days of the Week and Seasons

MONDAY

TUESDAY

WEDNESDAY

THURSDAY

FRIDAY **SATURDAY**

WONDERFUL (SUNDAY)

GROW (SPRING)

SUMMER

AUTUMN

COLD (WINTER)

Money and Ordinals

These signs also serve as ordinal numbers—i.e., first, second, third, etc.

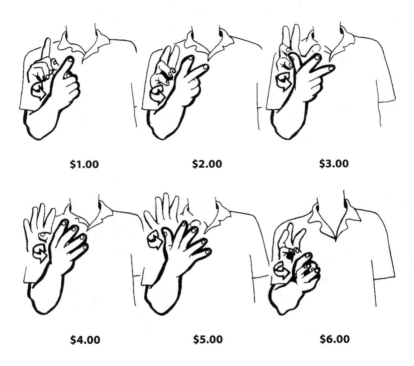

| $1.00 | $2.00 | $3.00 |

| $4.00 | $5.00 | $6.00 |

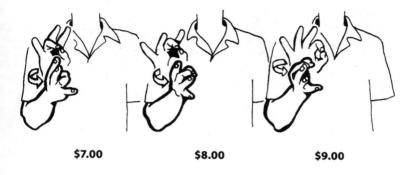

| $7.00 | $8.00 | $9.00 |

The sign DOLLAR is used when the amount is over nine dollars or when speaking specifically of a bill, as in "a dollar bill." As here:

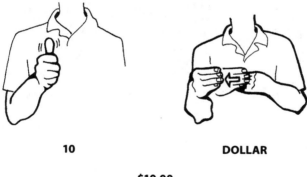

| 10 | DOLLAR |

$10.00

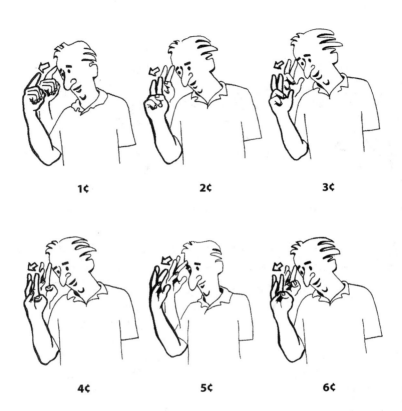

1¢   2¢   3¢

4¢   5¢   6¢

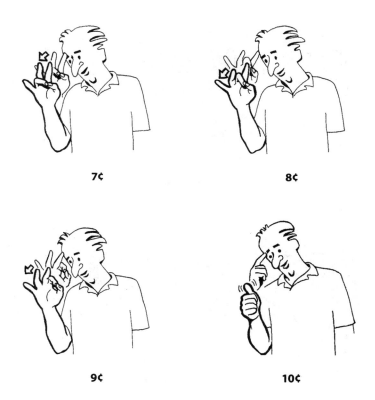

7¢

8¢

9¢

10¢

These signs are used only when speaking of these amounts by themselves, not when they are preceded by a dollar amount. For example, $3.09 would be signed as follows:

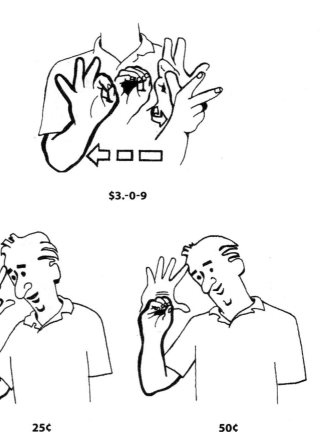

$3.-0-9

25¢   **50¢**

The same applies to the two individual cent signs above. Use them only when speaking of these amounts alone, and not with a dollar amount.

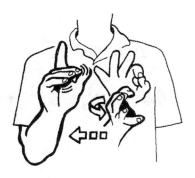

$9.-25

$1.-5-0

Appendix

The Manual Alphabet

When there is not a sign for an idea or concept, then fingerspelling using the manual alphabet occurs. Fingerspelling is used particularly with proper names; brand names; titles of books and movies; names of places and certain foods, etc. Mastery of fingerspelling can be achieved if you form good habits from the very beginning.

Here are some tips to follow when learning fingerspelling:

1. Relax your fingers and, in turn, your arm and shoulder. Tension will impede clear formation of the letters, or "handshapes," as they are called in the manual alphabet.
2. Let your arm hang down with your elbow to your side and your hand slightly in front of you. Do not allow your elbow to move away from your side and rise upward.
3. Do not try to fingerspell rapidly. It is important to maintain a constant rhythm, but do not bounce your hand. Speed will come naturally with time.
4. Pause for one-fourth of a beat at the end of a word if you are fingerspelling several words at a time.

5. Do not *say* the letters or words out loud or to yourself as you make them. Do not develop this habit, otherwise it will be exceedingly difficult to break once established. As you fingerspell a word, *mouth* the whole word. This is done especially with some Deaf people who have been taught to lipread words, not letters.
6. Practice with someone so you can gain experience reading fingerspelling.
7. In reading fingerspelling; look at the whole shape or configuration of the word rather than reading each individual letter or handshape.

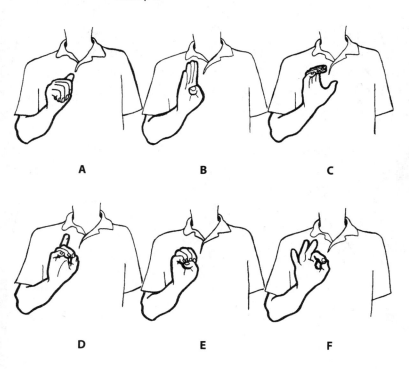

A   B   C

D   E   F

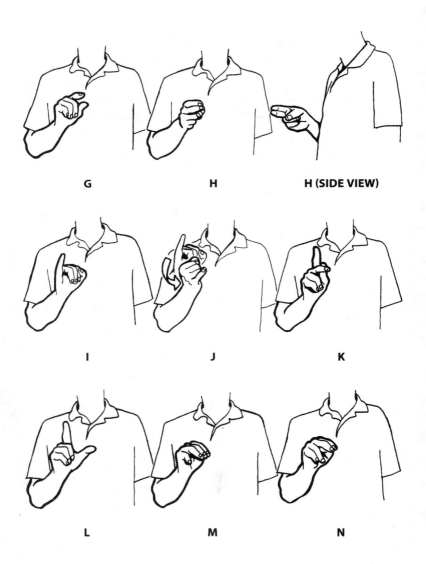

G   H   H (SIDE VIEW)

I   J   K

L   M   N

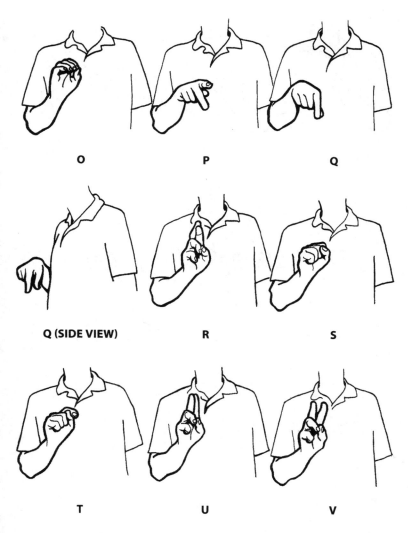

O

P

Q

Q (SIDE VIEW)

R

S

T

U

V

The sign for the letter *O* is the same as that for the number 0 (zero).

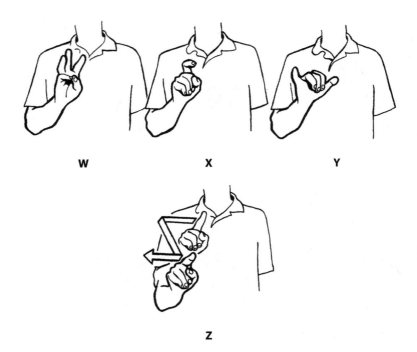

W   X   Y

Z